winner
michigan writers cooperative press
2023 poetry contest

THE SOUND
A CAR DOOR MAKES

Natalie Tomlin

Michigan Writers Cooperative Press
P. O. Box 2355
Traverse City, Michigan 49685

ISBN-13: 978-1-950744-13-8

Book cover by Amy Hansen
Book interior by Daniel Stewart

Contents

In the long journey out of the self,
There are many detours, washed-out interrupted raw places
Where the shale slides dangerously
And the back wheels hang almost over the edge
At the sudden veering, the moment of turning.

Theodore Roethke,
"Journey to the Interior"

The Sound a Car Door Makes

prose poems

Slams

I once heard on public radio that the sound a car door makes
when it slams is cooked up in some lab in Minneapolis—the more
expensive the car, the plusher the reverb. Techs delight most when
we passengers vibrate, when we feel as if we could hurtle toward
the moon, orbit roadkill and panhandlers completely untouched.
Bloomberg reported that Mercedes worked for decades to ensure
that all its cars, from a $115,000 S-CLASS limousine to a beat-up 1992
model, close with a "satisfying, vault-like thunk." To experience this
artistry, visit dealerships, valet lanes, parking structures that echo
after the movie ends, when each of our minds clicks shut. Wake early,
stand outside the high school at drop-off hour: rain on leaves, bullets
through velvet. And yet I suppose it all depends upon which side of
the door you're on.

Divorce, thirty years later

At the gas station, I swear I saw my father's hands, heard his shiny
brown shoes and the flashy way they would touch down on the curb,
as if to signal that this visit would be short. His leased suv landed
outside like a rare bird once a month, per the custody agreement.
Smooth jazz was always pumping when he picked me up, but the
last time we spoke over the phone, he made me promise to listen to
Taj Mahal. Will we ever get to listen to his crates of lps? To think
I make it sound as if he is no longer here. When I drive toward the
expressway, past twenty-four-hour diners hanging on like dried-out
barnacles, I hear him scoot into a vinyl booth, unfurl over our hour-
long lunches, an improvised song.

Body repair

The car emerged the same as before, yet somehow younger—
taillights sharp, pretty eyes and trunk waxed, spotless. The day
before, after the accident, I knelt and pulled a glittery splinter from
my son's leg. He now climbs a stripped-down Mustang in a lobby
and fear has nowhere to go: rain huddles near curbs as I drive home,
still not aware of the stickers studding my new yet secondhand
back window, madcap stickers one might expect in the window of
a teenager, someone like the blond boy who hit us, stormed from
his car yelling, *You could have made that yellow light!* I haul him and
the entire city onward, cars trailing like wicked toys on a string.
When will my hands, two bells, stop vibrating? As if to answer, the
Collision Center pops a survey into my email: *Were you completely
satisfied? Win a New Car!*

Headlights

Don't ask me how I ended up there, alone in woods fringing a cleft in the earth. Rumor had it the property was the Department of Natural Resource's dumping ground for deer that had been hit. Before the cops busted the party and everyone took off, I wandered from the bonfire to pee and lay down, the hooks of vodka and Mountain Dew pinning me to the ground. When I came to, I was alone. Smoke from the smothered fire had a ghostly sway, at least what I could see beyond my hand in front of my face.

I ran barefoot for what seemed like hours, stumbling over hills where RVs came to spin their tires, but it probably wasn't more than twenty minutes before I spotted headlights. At first, I wasn't very relieved, because I thought it could be the cops and I already had a "minor in possession" under my belt. But I got lucky—I ended up in a nice family's living room. Three a.m. and my screaming from over a mile away had woken them. My friends wouldn't answer the phone, so the cops drove me back to my apartment with black light Led Zeppelin posters. My best friend probably rolled over as I walked in, her back facing me, my voice leaking into her dream.

Dear Mr. Hicok

You'd be pleased to know that this summer, I wore cicadas as earrings. As they roiled, I wrote louder. Since I discovered you owned a tool and die shop, jigs, molds, and gaugers scramble out from under every rock I turn over. Ball bearings speed my thoughts, giddy with the possibility that in my lifetime I may have been transported by another thing stamped by you. Die maker sounds like "D'yer Maker," yet John Paul Jones disliked that song; it started out as a joke in the studio. What are cars, Mr. Hicok? Skulls we shine on Sundays?

This is it

1998. We stole it at night, running across a lawn we had scoped out beforehand. With a firm kick, I popped it out neatly and ran away with it under my arm like a football, never really breaking my stride. The runaway car was there, waiting. At first we thought we would start a collection, but something stopped us from progressing past three or four. My theory is we found the one that could not be topped. Sure, there was "Buy Now and Save," which communicated all that we hated, but when we found "This Is It" printed in bold letters on thick plastic and slid into the slot above the real estate "For Sale" sign, it became an unfurled fortune cookie message, a street sign I placed above the entrance to my apartment, a bumper sticker I propped in the back window of my Chevy Lumina, a thought bubble or caption or reminder or koan or epitaph that we once took to the bar, onto the dance floor to hold above our heads as we danced to Hard Knock Life and laughed and scanned the faces, hoping everyone would understand with us. We were nineteen and it was our dictum from the real estate gods and I would love to know where that sign went. But really, nothing was lost. We discovered it. Nothing can take it away.

Deprivation

Wikipedia says cul-de-sac is a synonym for "dead end," but I disagree;
I hear "lull," not "kill." When my son was three and a half, I drove in
loops to keep him from waking from his afternoon nap, peeked into
the rearview, which peeked into a little plastic mirror attached to the
middle backseat so I could catch a glimpse inside his meticulously
researched rear-facing car seat. We felt compelled to buy the CR-V
after we were rear-ended in our Civic, but even so, the University
of Wyoming found that two-adult households with children emit
over 25% more carbon dioxide than two-adult households without
children. Now Gabe has dropped his nap and we try to take the bus
everywhere. He stands up before the bus completely stops, strangers
reach out to keep him upright. On our way home from the bus stop,
we relearn walking and its lawlessness, that you can stop completely
when an acorn catches your eye or collapse without warning, sobbing
into the snowbank of late morning. And the CR-V? I never stopped
missing its pert blue paint.

Core

Seventeen: no one can strap me into this world. Deer hair flaps out of my door handle, a headlight dangles from its mangled socket on a bright green wire. Don't worry, the light still turns on: you should see how it sets the tops of the apple trees on fire. Thirty-seven: I finally have a driveway, a crab apple tree that sprays blossoms into the bluest sky. The sound of teeth in an apple when I don't see him: my son, the runner. My plucked flesh gripped in something's palm, thin juice pulsing: *At the core of a child is the crisp gasp of a mother.*

Ditch bouquet

Hazard lights counterpoint my heartbeat as I pick flowers from the ditch. One wears tiny white spikes to match the froth that comes when its stem finally snaps. Sharp with pollen, already wilting as I bouquet: cylindrical blazing star, abundant after fires.

The ride in the middle of the mall

was a boxy white pod and it was expensive; admission was maybe
two dollars in 1991. A metal door rolled down to close us in: carpeted
walls, a couple rows of couch seats you find in vans, a projector on
the ceiling showing us what it would look like if we were riding
a roller coaster right at that moment, our pod slowly tilting as
we clicked up a hill. We wore seatbelts, which helped when the
hydraulics kicked in and the roller coaster detached from the track,
ascended and dodged asteroids. It was the place to be. One girl said
to her friend as they walked by after getting their ears pierced at
Claire's Boutique, *We should try that sometime.*

Ruin porn

This House Is Being Watched was what I wanted to see most, those giant signs on half-charred houses, two cartoon eyes appearing when my headlights met them. Nineteen or twenty when I drove a little under an hour from my hometown to cruise West Grand Boulevard. Along with Woodward, it was the widest river of concrete I had ever seen. Rows of streetlights burned out, the night a tunnel. Does it matter that I didn't know I was entertaining myself? Two decades would pass before some fifty thousand city residents would band together to nearly eliminate Devil's Night arson. Back then, I knew nothing.

Sidewalks

They are treating their cars like they did in high school, one reporter wrote. I admit I Googled "COVID divorce," but we were fine; I just wanted to know if it was normal to feel as if we were living inside an iron lung. After the lockdown, dust had settled on the dashboard, the streets were empty; I took off in an ambulance or a jet or nothing, a cyborg at one with her automobile as she swooped over rolling hills, taking note of which stores had curbside. And yet everyone on the neighborhood Facebook wanted to know what was up with all the speeding, cars even hopping curbs during drag races. Second telephone pole down in a month, one just a few feet from where my son rode this bike. I had always thought sidewalks were sacred.

Dear Mr. Iacocca

Tell me about the golden mean and I will tell you how I totaled my
k-car at age sixteen. Tonight, glitter bombs drop beyond my middle-
class trees and I should be happy: it's the Fourth of July. Romantic
but not true, you said, of the rumor that you had been christened
Lido, after your parent's honeymoon in the Lido region of Italy.
Until I had insomnia the night I found out you died, I didn't know
you endorsed George W., then Kerry; that in '07 you called out the
"bozos" who couldn't build a hybrid. Tonight, tell me about the
middle road, bankruptcy, knowing Chrysler would eventually come
back. Don't be any type of leader and take me back to '93, to that
olive oil–based margarine product you founded: in a boardroom,
taking Olivio on a warm spoon, prepping to appear on TV, a faint
aftertaste on the roof of your mouth.

Beck would have approved

of our detour, or perhaps not. I pretended it was all hilarious while we had dinner in Ann Arbor, an hour away from where the show was happening, just outside of Detroit. But we missed the *Odelay* tour. What the hell would we tell the next generation, and the generation after that? There was a time when you could drive anywhere and we did and got lost out of our minds.

Toy designers take note

Age five, motor skills. A Hot Wheels track called Shark Park. Winding ramp before the jaws snap and the shark says, "Mmm, tasty," in an Eddie Van Halen voice, but Gabe was finished with it after two weeks. Age two, matching. Battery-powered puzzle with sounds. Firetruck, airplane, each with a tiny handle, but no on-off switch. Sometimes late at night, a police siren calls out from the basement toy box, triggered for no reason. Age one, cause and effect. Plastic car shape filled with five chunky gears. In the center of each gear is the face of a smiling child. Turn the gears and the pastel heads turn, but not from side to side. Chin over scalp, balls rolling out into the street.

Butterfly

That night I thought I wanted to die: I hit a patch of ice on I-94, emerged from the brittle edges of a 360, and, for nearly two weeks before my twenty-fourth birthday, basked.

How exactly Joan of Arc traveled

wasn't detailed much on Wikipedia, except in a painting of her
riding a white horse while wearing a suit of dark gold. And I'm not
doing anything heroic, but I think of her anyway, gripping a pole in
each hand, my sleeping baby strapped to my chest and feet wide as I
brace against the hurtling train, along with a blind man and two kids
passing out concert fliers. On the Chicago Brown Line the summer
scientists pinpointed twenty-seven states of emotion—I am holiday
lights unfurling after being wound tight in boxes all summer. Bed
bugs are rumored to live in the fabric-covered seats, but I no longer
want my Honda and its uninterrupted dream. *This is the last stop. All
passengers must vacate and reboard to continue riding.* And now pacing
the Kimball station. Cars below, braking and gassing, while I keep
watch, elevated.

The man who walked

The lot was teeming when I found him, untethered and heading north on the shoulder, against traffic. *No one looks*, he had yelled back after he cashed a few empties at Love's Travel Stop, letting us customers know that we hung turns without properly checking. Because of him, I now revere crosswalks, their resolve, their distress: how faded they can become, like a child's rained-out sidewalk drawings.

Horse-drawn streetcar

In use from 1870 to 1890, before electric-powered streetcars, it was restored in cadmium yellow, Paris green, and vermilion glaze, with the number 49 in carmine and ultramarine blue. The towering chestnut brown horse, nearly as tall as the car itself turned toward me as Gabe climbed and reached for the reins. "Do Not Climb," said a sign next to the sealed windows, and I could imagine myself inside there, hands folded on my lap, eyes focused at a socially appropriate focal point. A citizen in a community of commuters, not a driver of a single passenger car. I had always thought that option was stolen when General Motors bought up all the streetcars but later found out that streetcars died from a confluence of white flight and our preference for autonomy. "Don't forget your free parking pass," a clerk said as we headed out of the Grand Rapids Public Museum after we passed a towering replica of the state of Michigan encrusted in metal: *If you're like most people, you collect your old license plates, even display them in your garage. That's because driving holds powerful memories for us.* Outside, we choose between the parking structure and the Grand River, flowing stealth below the overpass. "Far-Flowing Water," the Ottawa people call it, or "Owashtanong." I love hearing its current burn, that wayward road of gray flames. Listening as it mocks asphalt. Listen.

Sources

Bloomberg, "vault-like thunk": James Tarmy, "Mercedes Doors Have a Signature Sound: Here's How," Bloomberg, August 5, 2014, https://www.bloomberg.com/news/articles/2014-08-05/mercedes-doors-have-a-signature-sound-here-s-how.

University of Wyoming, carbon dioxide: "Economists Find Carbon Footprint Grows with Parenthood," Science Daily, April 15, 2020, https://www.sciencedaily.com/releases/2020/04/200415152921.htZ.

Angels' night: "Detroit Angels' Night: Data behind This Year's Record-Low Fire Count," MLive, November 2, 2012, https://www.mlive.com/news/detroit/2012/11/detroit_angels_night_data_behi.html.

Restored in cadmium yellow: Veronica Kandl, "Restoration of the Public Museum's Horsedrawn Streetcar, History Grand Rapids.org, Grand Rapids Historical Commission, February 14, 2009, www.historygrandrapids.org/photoessay/1675/restoration-of-the-public-muse.

White flight and consumer preference for autonomy: Mark Henricks, "The GM Trolley Conspiracy: What Really Happened," CBS News, updated September 2, 2010, https://www.cbsnews.com/news/the-gm-trolley-conspiracy-what-really-happened/.

Acknowledgments

"Journey to the Interior," copyright © 1961 by Beatrice Roethke, Administratrix of the Estate of Theodore Roethke. Copyright © 1966 and renewed 1994 by Beatrice Lushington; from *Collected Poems* by Theodore Roethke. Used by permission of Doubleday, an imprint of the Knopf Doubleday Publishing Group, a division of Penguin Random House LLC. All rights reserved.

"Dear Mr. Hicok" appeared in *Dunes Review*, Summer 2017.

"This Is It" appeared in *River Teeth* online, Summer 2017.

"Dear Mr. Iacocca" appeared in *Essay Daily*, Summer 2021.

My gratitude to Kathi McGookey for her generous guidance and encouragement as I worked on this collection.

About the Judge

Michigan Writers Cooperative Press would like to express our thanks to Jennifer Sperry Steinorth. Jennifer's books include *A Wake with Nine Shades* (2019) and *Her Read, A Graphic Poem* (2021), recipient of *Foreword Review*'s bronze prize in poetry and Texas Institute of Letters' Fred Whitehead Award for Design. She lectures at the University of Michigan and is a 2023-2024 Beinecke Fellow at Yale, conducting research for a biography of C.D. Wright. Scholarly work on Wright is forthcoming from the University of Michigan Press and elsewhere and her poetry appears or is forthcoming from *The Cincinnati Review, Denver Quarterly Review, Kenyon Review, Missouri Review, Pleiades, Plume, RHINO* and *TriQuarterly.* An alum of Interlochen Arts Academy, her interdisciplinary approach to language is drawn from years as a classical dancer and a decade in architectural design and construction. She has served on the Michigan Writers Board of Directors and divides her time between Ann Arbor and Traverse City, Michigan.

About the Author

Natalie Tomlin is a freelance writer and editor. Her writing has appeared in many magazines, including *Belt, Dunes Review, The Hopper,* and *Split Rock Review.* Her nonfiction has been nominated for Best of Net, the Pushcart Prize, and was selected as notable in *The Best American Essays 2018.* She has a passion for writing criticism, especially when highlighting Michigan poets, and her reviews can be found at *Diode, Grist: A Journal of the Literary Arts, New Pages,* and elsewhere. Her journalism on education, culture, and food has appeared at *Michigan Radio, Literary Mama,* and elsewhere. A former waitress, high school teacher, and college adjunct, she has taught writing at DePaul University and Eastern Michigan University. She grew up on Lake Huron and now lives in Grand Rapids, Michigan with her family, where she's at work on a collection of essays on parenting and protecting Michigan's flora and fauna.

About Michigan Writers Cooperative Press

This book was published in the spring of 2023 in a signed edition of 100 copies.

This chapbook is part of the Cooperative Series of the Michigan Writers Small Press Project, which was launched in 2005 to give members of Michigan Writers, Inc. a new avenue to publication. All of the chapbooks in this series are an author's first book in that genre. The Coop Press shoulders the publishing costs for the first edition, and writers share the marketing and promotional responsibilities in return for the prestige of being published by a press that prints only carefully selected manuscripts.

Chapbook length manuscripts of poetry, short stories, and essays are solicited each year from members and adjudicated by a panel of experienced writers and a judge who is a specialist in a particular genre. For more information, please visit www.michwriters.org.

MICHIGAN WRITERS is an open-membership organization dedicated to providing opportunities for networking, professional growth, and publication for writers of all ages and skill levels in Northwest Michigan and beyond.

MANAGING EDITORS Gail Wallace Bozzano

BOOK DESIGN: Amy Hansen, Daniel Stewart

Other Titles Available
from Michigan Writers Cooperative Press

The Grace of the Eye by Michael Callaghan
Trouble With Faces by Trinna Frever
Box of Echoes by Todd Mercer
Beyond the Reach of Imagination by Duncan Spratt Moran
The Grass Impossibly by Holly Wren Spaulding
The Chocolatier Speaks of his Wife by Catherine Turnbull
Dangerous Exuberance by Leigh Fairey
Point of Sand by Jaimien Delp
Hard Winter, First Thaw by Jenny Robertson
Friday Nights the Whole Town Goes to the Basketball Game
        by Teresa J. Scollon
Seasons for Growing by Sarah Baughman
Forking the Swift by Jennifer Sperry Steinorth
The Rest of Us by John Mauk
Kisses for Laura by Joan Schmeichel
Eat the Apple by Denise Baker
First Risings by Michael Hughes
Fathers and Sons by Bruce L. Makie
Exit Wounds by Jim Crockett
The Solid Living World by Ellen Stone
Bitter Dagaa by Robb Astor
Crime Story by Kris Kuntz
Michaela by Gabriella Burman
Supposing She Dreamed This by Gail Wallace Bozzano
Line and Hook by Kevin Griffin
And Sarah His Wife by Christina Diane Campbell
Proud Flesh by Nancy Parshall
Angel Rides a Bike by Margaret Fedder
Ink by Kathleen Pfeiffer
What Will You Teach Her? by Megan Klco Kellner
Bluetongue and Other Michigan Stories by Ryan Shek
The Mountain Ash by Kathleen Rabbers
This Blue Earth by Sharon Bippus
Upstairs, Listening by Melida LePere
Twinkies by Kathleen Quigley
The Sound a Car Door Makes by Natalie Tomlin

Michigan
WRITERS

www.ingramcontent.com/pod-product-compliance
Lightning Source LLC
Chambersburg PA
CBHW061501210726
48287CB00007B/2615